NATIONAL
GEOGRAPHIC

Crittercam

Andrew Einspruch

Contents

Crittercam

What is it like to be a wild animal? What do they see? You can find out using Crittercam. "Crittercam" is short for "critter camera." A Crittercam is a special video camera that scientists put on, or attach, to an animal. The camera films everything the animal does.

▼ This seal is wearing a Crittercam on its back.

Scientists attach a Crittercam to
a wild animal. Then they let the animal
go. The camera records
how the animal lives.

Crittercam can show a whale diving
deep into the dark ocean. It can show
a group of lions hunting. It
can also show how penguins live
in their icy world. When Crittercam
is attached to a seal, scientists
can learn how seals behave
underwater.

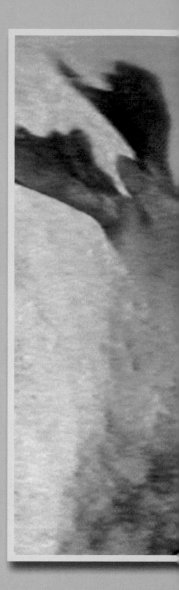

▲ Crittercam shows a seal in the ocean.

Making a Crittercam

Each Crittercam is made especially for the animal that will wear it. The camera must be sturdy because it often gets bumped while it is attached to the animal. It must also be waterproof in case the animal goes in the ocean or splashes across a river.

▼ This diagram shows the different parts of a Crittercam.

Video Tape Deck

Housing

Antenna

Hydrophone

Lens

CRITTERCAM

Environmental Sensors

Computer

Batteries

Headlights

Crittercam

O-Ring Seals

Mount

Length: 10 inches
Weight: 1.5 kilos

Seal

This penguin isn't ▶ bothered by its Crittercam.

Scientists make sure the camera won't hurt the animal. They want the animal to ignore the camera. This is because scientists want to record the animal's normal life. If wearing the camera bothers the animal, the animal's behavior might change.

Attaching Crittercam

Scientists attach Crittercams in different ways on different animals. They use suction cups to attach Crittercams to whales. Scientists attach Crittercams to penguins using a special harness that the bird wears like a backpack.

▼ Crittercams with suction cups are used on animals that live in the ocean.

▲ A whale wears a Crittercam with a suction cup.

Suction cup

▲ Scientists recover a Crittercam that has fallen off an ocean animal.

Removing Crittercam

Crittercams are made to fall off the animal after a certain amount of time. The Crittercam sends out a signal so scientists can find it after it has fallen off the animal. After the scientists find the Crittercam, they watch what the Crittercam has recorded.

Penguin Crittercam

Scientists have attached Crittercams to penguins. The cameras show how the penguins live in their frozen world. The Crittercams showed the penguins swimming in the freezing Antarctic water.

Scientists learned that the penguins do not always dive down to catch their fish. Sometimes they dive down so they can look up! The penguins look up at the bottom of the white ice. Fish are easy to see against this white background.

Crittercam shows ▶
what the ice looks
like to a penguin
in the water.

◀ A penguin dives
into a hole in
the ice.

A penguin swims ▶
up towards the ice
to catch a fish.

Whale Crittercam

Scientists have attached Crittercams to sperm whales. These animals dive deep into the ocean looking for food. They go where it is cold and dark.

Crittercams made for whales have "headlights" so they can be used in the dark. They have sound recorders, too. The Crittercams can also measure how deep the whales dive.

Scientists have heard sperm whales talk to each other using clicks, squeals, and rumbling sounds. They also learned that the whales bump each other hard enough to rub off bits of skin. Some scientists think this could be how the whales clean each other.

▲ Scientists move closer to a whale
so they can attach a Crittercam.

▲ Scientists watch a whale swim away
after they have attached a Crittercam.

Lions were the first wild land animals to wear Crittercams. They wore the cameras on collars around their necks. Using Crittercam, scientists could see a group of lions hunting together.

Scientists didn't know how they would keep the lenses on Crittercams clean when they were on the lions. The lions solved this problem for the scientists. When they licked each other clean, the lions licked the camera lenses clean, too.

▲ A lion wears a Crittercam on a collar.

◀ Crittercam shows a mother lion's view of her cub.

Lots More to Learn

Scientists are working on new Crittercams. They want to make the cameras smaller, lighter, and more powerful. They also want to study many more animals.

Imagine Crittercams on eagles soaring through the air. Imagine Crittercams on bears living in the forest. Imagine Crittercams on dolphins racing across the ocean. There's lots more for us to learn using Crittercams.